ALWAYS ME:
Affirmations for Incredible Kids

Always Me: Affirmations for Incredible Kids
Published by Samantha Shekian Publishing

Text copyright © Samantha Shekian
Illustrations copyright © Ayan Mansoori
All rights reserved.

Cover design by Aeyshaa

Contact the publisher for special discounts on bulk purchases. For more information, contact samanthashekian@gmail.com

Reproduction of this book in any manner, in whole or in part, without the publisher's written permission is prohibited.

Print Paperback ISBN: 978-1-7390298-8-3
Print Hardcover ISBN: 978-1-7390298-9-0
eBook ISBN: 978-1-0692860-0-0

Second print edition.

Disclaimer: This information is not meant to be a substitute for professional advice. If you have con- cerns about a child's wellbeing, please seek professional help.

Dedication

To all my beautiful, incredible, and kind students, thank you for inspiring me to write my first book. This was possible because of YOU!

To all my loved ones, I can't thank you enough for your constant support, encouragement, and love. Thank you for cheering me on.

Hello, friends!

This book is all about affirmations. An affirmation is like a seed of positive thoughts. You know how plants need water and sunlight to grow big and strong?

Are you ready to say an affirmation together? I'll say it first, and then you can repeat it after me. Ready?

I am ME!

I am beautiful.

I am beautiful.

I am smart!

I am capable.

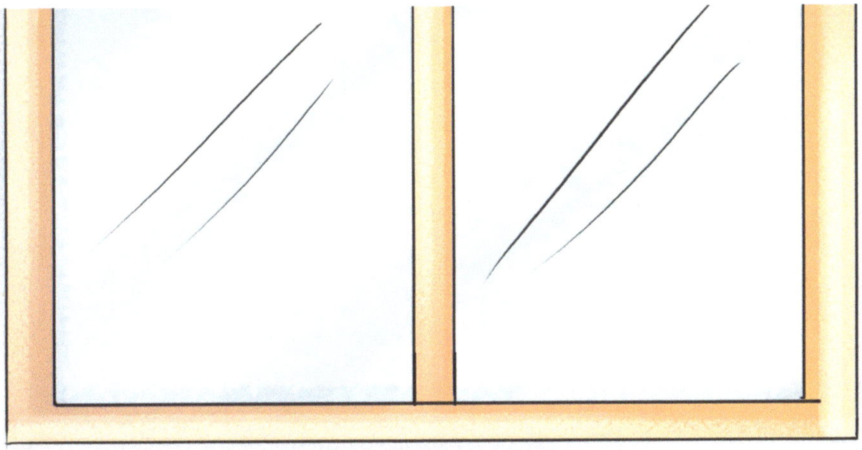

I am kind!

I am a leader.

I am responsible.

I am proud of myself!

Here are some questions to ask the children in your life:

- What does it mean to be YOU?
- What are some qualities that you love about yourself?
- What makes you feel beautiful?
- What makes you feel smart?
- What makes you feel capable?
- When and how can you be kind?
- What makes you feel like a leader?
- What makes you a good friend?
- What great things can you do?
- What brings you joy?
- Describe a time you were silly.
- What does it mean to be responsible? How are you responsible for yourself?
- You ARE important! What's important to you?
- You ARE enough! What does it mean to be enough?
- What are you proud of?

About the Author

Samantha Shekian is an esteemed early elementary educator currently employed with the New York City Department of Education. Throughout her teaching journey, Samantha has instilled the practice of daily affirmations in her classrooms, which has become a cherished and empowering ritual for her students. By fostering feelings of capability and strength, these affirmations have left a positive and lasting impact on the young minds she nurtures.

www.ingramcontent.com/pod-product-compliance
Lightning Source LLC
LaVergne TN
LVHW070256080526
838200LV00091B/356